VIA FOLIOS 96

Praise for *Via Incanto: Poems from the Darkroom*

In poems haunted by the dead "Photographer God" Marisa Frasca takes up the now almost forgotten voice of a gifted storyteller — part spell, alive with detail, she transports Sicily to the New World. Poems, like some passions, can be dangerous — eating an artichoke delicately "so needles won't stick in my throat." Loss is countered by the pulse of all that is wild — an ocean, a volcano, a gull feather, blood oranges, mandolins. These are layered poems, where ancient songs infuse the modern. Frasca is bold and she can see in the dark.

— Anne Marie Macari

Here is a writer who knows that the soul and its sensibility are made not only by one's own personal history, but by a collective and often difficult past that enters the body, the bones, the psyche. In *Via Incanto: Poems from the Darkroom*, Frasca depicts a knottier set of family roots, a legacy that includes violence, brutality, and all-too-human vanities. Precision of detail ("Never saw my kid whipped with oxtail dipped in salt and fat…") and a calm steady gaze ("The woman with downcast eyes hurries her limping…") promise the reader an authenticity that a more sentimentalized or apologetic view of the past couldn't bear forth. Here is a writer who trusts language and image to suggest cadence and music, and draws from harshness, a sustaining beauty.

— Lia Purpura

Via Incanto
Poems from the Darkroom

Marisa Frasca

BORDIGHERA PRESS

Library of Congress Control Number: 2014944619.

Printed in the United States.

Published by
BORDIGHERA PRESS
John D. Calandra Italian American Institute
25 West 43rd Street, 17th Floor
New York, NY 10036

VIA FOLIOS 96
ISBN 978-1-59954-076-4

For Raffaela (Lina) Lauria   For Salvatore (Turiddu) Frasca
(1924-2000)   (1910-1962)

In memoriam

Acknowledgements

Thanks to the editors of the following publications in which these poems —some in different versions or with different titles have appeared or are forthcoming:

Embroidered Stories Anthology: Interpreting Women's Domestic Needlework from the Italian Diaspora: "Canto for a Quilter"

Veils, Halos and Shackles Anthology: International Poetry on the Abuse and Oppression of Women: "Licking Sardines" and "Catena in Black Shawl"

Sweet Lemons II Anthology: "Tight Tight Like Always"

5AM: "Raffaela at Eighteen"

VIA: "Ferragosto"

VIA: "Stritti Stritti Comu Sempri" with English translation "Tight Tight Like Always"

Adanna Journal: "Pink Moon Child"

Feile-Festa: "Quannu Chiuveva Petali Russi e Aranciuni" with English translation "When it Rained Red and Orange Petals"

12th Street: "Aranci Sanguigni Siciliani" with English translation "Sicilian Blood Oranges"

12th Street: "Meeting at MoMa"

Italian American Writers.com: "E Lucevan Le Stelle"

TABLE OF CONTENTS

I

Discordanza   3

Aranci Sanguigni Siciliani   4

Sicilian Blood Oranges   5

In the Darkroom   6

Transcendence in Thunder Hole   8

Down Rocky Point Road   9

Providence on Paradise Island   10

The Viewer's Eye   12

Gust of Wind   13

A Voice Suddenly Said   14

II

Licking Sardines   17

Depth of Field   18

Kayaking Peconic Bay   21

Spinnannu ppi li Labbra D'avutri   22

Yearning for the Lips of Others   23

Sonnet for a Girl   24

Pink Moon Child   25

That Jasmine Twig   29

I Wanted to Show You   30

Cafeteria Carpet   31

New World Names & Notions   32

Photo of Hunchback Woman on the Battlefield   34

III

Transforming the I   37

Santuzza, bitter bride, encounters Ms. Alien

   researching Sicily's 20th century marriage customs   38

More Sicilian Sickness   41

Ferragosto   42

Amore Muto   43

Folle, Furtive Little Night Dream   44

The College Boyfriend   45

Comma in the Sky   46

Meeting at MoMA   47

Disposable Goods   48

Raffaela at Eighteen   49

Quannu Chiuveva Petali Russi e Aranciuni   52

When it Rained Red and Orange Petals   53

New Wine in November   54

E Lucevan Le Stelle   55

Filament Yarns   56

Ars Poetica   57

IV

Via Incanto   61

Stritti Stritti Comu Sempri   62

Tight Tight Like Always   63

Braided Tree   66

Catena in Black Shawl   67

Canto for a Quilter   69

Petra Panayotis   70

The Water Episode   71

Athena to a Dreamer   73

Aurora   74

The Emerald Dress   75

When All Grew Silent   77

Don Paolo's Myth   79

September Equinox   81

Ask the Sun for a Face of Petals   82

ABOUT THE AUTHOR   83

I

Discordanza

I need my mind back. Think and know only in part. Leaf through
yellowing letters.
We began as musical sounds
like a voice that persuades.

I need my mind back. Every fool on earth knows
deferred dreams
feel as amputees home from war feel,

hands reach for phantom limbs.
My eyes and lips fall through the world.
I need my heart back, today. I couldn't leave,

heart clogged, feet stalled at the threshold—door barred
by a furious storm
piling up ice to the peephole. Clocked 11:59

we stopped writing *sweet dreams.*
500 lbs. of artillery lifted   my shoulders relaxed.
I need here & now, to see morning again. Pages fall onto my lap:

For the wildest dance of my life—For the great ones
For those we never love in flesh & bone
eternally we love

maddened in exile.
Close the desk drawer gently.
Take the dog for a two-mile run.

Aranci Sanguigni Siciliani

Ogni vota ca vinia lu sangu
mi dicevi
nun lavarti
la testa specialmenti
ti fa mali
E n'avutra cosa ancora—
nun tuccari
li pianti—li pianti siccanu—
morinu—quannu hai
li cosi
li to` cosi

Teni li gammi
stritti—
l'occhi n'terra—
nun fissari
L'omini virinu—
sciaranu
lu nostru gridu silinziusu
d'accuppiamentu

Ogni vota ca vinia lu sangu
virevu aranci cunciuti
sanguigni Siciliani
sbattiri n'terra
Li pigghiavu a cauci
ci rumpevu li denti
fin ca lu sangu
fineva di scurriri

Sicilian Blood Oranges

Every time I bled
you said
don't wash
especially your head
it's bad for you
And another thing —
don't touch
the plants — plants wilt —
die — when you have
the things
your things

Tighten
those legs —
lower those eyes —
don't stare
Men can see —
smell
our silent mating calls

Every time I bled
I saw oranges
ripe Sicilian blood oranges
hit the ground
I kicked their teeth
until the blood
stopped flowing

In the Darkroom

Table height between father's legs I watched swan-like poses
of the effeminate man our village called *Little Woman*
who saved his money so once a year for *Carnevale* he could dress
in tulle and white organdy. He took off his farmer's shoes,
tip-toed in ballerina slippers down Via Cavour, a white cloud,
elegantissimo, blowing kisses

and those townspeople dressed in Pierrot pantaloons
and Colombina crinolines blew kisses back. For three days
and nights every risen angel and inner demon
celebrated victory. Unmasked dreams came to Frasca Studio
with the confidence of seasoned actors who postponed
tomorrow's sunup to sundown whistling to their picks and axes
so as not to think of rest.

Brides and funerals with bands led by open cymbals,
feet about to step, convened inside the darkroom's
one red bulb and heavy curtains that kept out light.
Father showed me how to retouch negatives, erase
hand calluses, facial warts, aging lines —
improvised tool — pencil with point-sculpted razor
tied to its tip. He scratched away

singing Verdi and Puccini. Two skilled strokes
put a sparkle back to someone's eyes.

He straightened noses if they weren't too crooked.
Customers said Signor Frasca was Jesus
fixing the deformed; others called him
"The Photographer God." What mystery the dark!

Black-red space flecked with 8x10 paper, developer, vapor,
blurs slowly ritualized hair, brows,
mouths—the displaced, the incomplete,
the made new
superimposed and piled together in chorus.

Transcendence in Thunder Hole

I hike down drunk from eating blueberries
where Peregrine falcons nest on open cliffs
overlooking the rugged Acadia coast—

drunk on scent of bayberry,
to stone walls where bees make love
to the salt-spray rose. I reach to touch

the rocks of Thunder Hole—
their texture—sculpted, serrated, jagged?
Divinely hammered replies Michelangelo

kneeling beside me in faded orange T—
camouflaged backpack initialed M.B.,
speaking English flawlessly, looking cool

as the Maine Moose in the beaver pond
who also caught my eye on the way down

Down Rocky Point Road

Behind the dead end sign a stairway
leads to L.I. Sound, rocks rising so high
you'll think Capri or Gibraltar. It's early fall
and the whole night is mine.

I'll be leaning on the boulder cave
—low tide by the water's edge—
eyes expectant. That sea out there
is ours, and when it swells and wind sweeps
our barefoot tracks, we'll glide
in water curls like children
who ran away from home.

Will you walk with me thinking only of now?
I'll forget the hard times, the ghostly
house, the weary stillness of the husband
and his wife—till dawn brings
boys with fishing poles
swinging down Rocky Point Road.

Providence on Paradise Island

March 18 between Saint Patrick's blessings
and Saint Joseph's *zeppole*. How could we fail?
We paid for a bullion broth reception,
airline tickets, put $300 in Maspeth Bank.
We put our heads on stained pillows by a grimy
window with parking lot view of howling dogs
in gang-heat. We shut the lights—the carpet smelled
of mold—switched them on—piss streaks
on peeled walls. The sheets stunk of rancid milk
and old grilled cattle. Frank the travel agent
had sworn Paradise Island was across the street.
How were we to know—twenty one and twenty four,
immigrants still learning to pronounce consommé—
on a plane but once. I forced a laugh.
But piracy, slavery, smuggled rot assembled
inside me, and neither of us spoke. Next night
we walked late to cross a bridge,
to reach a solitary beach of coral. The moon shone;
we tangled around her. Heaven was damp skin
and burning tongues—everywhere the longest
light welcomed. I watched you kneel to smooth
our bed of coral, pull me down in breaths of open, slow
you entered slow and skilled and unafraid
as your fingers picked me clean. Slow lasted
as rivers flow certain of a future. We smelled

of nature pools—newborn puddles rain had carved
on sand like a benediction. On Paradise Island we laid
our love down for the next forty years, and all
the Bahamas celebrated independence from the British
that precious year—1973—passed in true faith.

The Viewer's Eye

A lotus brooch in the middle of an artichoke hairdo, full lips slightly parted; languid almond eyes said I'm a woman. For years the large black and white portrait hung above the couch in father's studio that doubled as our living room. I first found my little button as I stared at Vanda one afternoon while the family napped. I knew not where Vanda ended and I began each time I passed the couch, looked up at her—saw my eyes in hers. Father brought her with us to America, but after he died, she looked a little more bruised each time we moved—once to escape his blood vomited on the bathroom floor, twice for being robbed. I think Mother forgot her in some corner of a Brooklyn apartment with four rail-road rooms—next to the dead plant next to the flame stitch donated couch. In a footed bathtub in the kitchen we washed our clothes, and a Frigidaire dry as sawdust stored our hand-embroidered percale sheets. Vanda has clung to my mind's glassbowl of dust for fifty years—like a whirling scirocco.

Gust of Wind

That gull feather
I found in silted sand
& slipped under your hat's brim
Sometimes comes in fits
It flew away
You ran after it
It flew away
There's no point you said
We can't outrun the wind
Hush   baby   hush
It's just the way the planet breathes
Around salt waters of our world
Though I inhaled the gust
When your eyes windowed
When we were almost lovers
We were almost lovers

A Voice Suddenly Said

You will see a second time
when cataracts burden your eyes —
when you need to drown a sorrow
or set sail for coastal cities of joy,
lies, incantations, unsuspected
longings never sung aloud.

You will see a second time
your contradictions, appetites,
dark rooms of your mind.
It will be what you must do
alone, in a continent of silence.
Heed the pact—serve the art—

and it will flame your heart's
enthusiasm. Bitter will spin
and turn sweet, and sweet
fling toward bitter.
You will see a second time
what you so little expect.

II

Licking Sardines

But I was never beaten when I looked up at the sky
Never wore black shawl over my head—black drowning my eyes
Never mended socks with fingers bloodied by thorny fields
Never sucked flat caps before they'd toss sardine skeletons to lick
Never was forced down on four legs—couldn't kick
tied like a sheep
Was never beast with ripped hind
Never had ribs cracked when I was swollen with child
Never cleaned dirt floors with my hair—kid hanging on teat
Never saw my kid whipped with oxtail dipped in salt and fat
Why is my soul trapped in my mothers' Sicilian hell?

Depth of Field

One day the art demon launched its assault on her
who grew more crooked every day
like the pine tree in her backyard
trying to avoid electric wires. Sun
melted like wax and dark swallowed her
in one great gulp. In the annals of earth
she was pronounced guilty of forgetting cells
of her own heart. Who is accusing?
In the dark it's hard to know.

Father, is that you dangling the red light bulb
behind my eyes from your grave? Why
do you come so late in fountainrush of thought
rising like an Oligarch Christ?
I don't have 50 years. It takes that long
to become a poet. Why come so late
without fitting orientation?

Had I not loved enough or cried enough,
dug deep enough into my river bloodstream
after we crossed the Atlantic and huddled close
on the deck of the Christopher Columbus.
On that big ship our faces small and filled with hope
looked towards America, looked up
at clouds that would bring such rain.

A calm, deluding, ravenous sea
feigned gentleness and promise,
fragmented your student of the clouds
when your master hand let go.
Who is this hyphenated woman now
never mastering either tongue, a migratory bird circling round the new and old.
Could you instruct me how to be filled
with the absolute of vitality and mind.
I seemed to have sacrificed one and the other — decades
passed lost in continual sleep. While the earth chewed your bones
I survived without voice — soul suspended between two shores.

Now the ground gives, swallows
my nine year old mind and late adulthood body. I am afraid
to discover what I am, am not, what I lack, what I might have been —
fever to speculate stabs at my chest and I stretch
headlong into the dark, you see, I approach
learning like a child, invent
you're sending messages. What will I say
with the thoughts of a child?   What to do with this fascination

but narrate beginnings before the world
became criminal murdering love —
            love at a faraway table exposed — the way
our teeth close around tasty bits of steamed artichoke leaves
until we get down to the core and you savor
the last translucent purple thistle —
with such delicacy and care you spoon scrape the choke —
so needles won't stick in my throat —

dip the prized portion in olive oil, tenderly raise the heart to my mouth
and I enter eternity—hold tight, hold tight a mouthful of heart.

Kayaking Peconic Bay

Early morning mist veils Rabbit Lane's cottages
overlaid in shingles peeled by sea air—Bug Lighthouse
squats in the distance. Under Orient's overpass

we're inside Monet's *Soleil Levant*—but this blue-green
inlet has marshes, poletops with osprey nests,
black herons perch on rocks, muscles latching on—

almost noon, sun high, haze lifted—nothing moves
along this liquid path. We glide our kayaks onto sand,
where Bay meets Sound we meet again under a shady pine—

unwrap bread, olive spread, wine intensifies
everything. How can this be? Not a soul here—
only smooth stones white as eggs, blue, beryl,

amber sea glass. Someday no one will drink
from glass bottles any more. Only this sea glass
in our hands will attest to a day of fugue—when the Bay

was silenced by the sun. The gulls, little crabs watched
you—that old look in your eyes after all these years—living
driftwood splayed in salty air, a scent—half yours, half sea.

Spinnannu ppi li Labbra D'avutri

Idda pratica forti ppi perdiri l'accentu,
aRRotola paRoli AmiRicani chiu` di quantu necessaRiu

'nta lu scuru cimiteru assitata cu l'amici
tra petri tumbali, fumannu cigaretti Marlboro russi,

cantannu in armunia comu *Beach Boys*,
facennu sirinata alli morti.

E comu li morti ca camminanu invisibbili,
spinnanu ancora ppi lu puturi di parola,

la picciutedda senza scola—na scarpa lassata 'nta na riva,
scarpa 'nta l'avutra—trova lu trenu di 14 Strati,

l'atra strata Bleecker, cu vistina macchiata,
scavusa, paci e sciuri pittati 'nta na guancia—*O Man!*

The times they are a-changin, ma nenti,
nenti e` *cool*. Cu e` Rosa Parks? Dutt. King,

NAM? Cui? Cu cci 'nsigna a vasari cu la lingua,
a ballari u lentu lentu, cu la chiama diavula vistuta blu?

Yearning for the Lips of Others

She practices hard to lose her accent,
Rolls AmeRican woRds moRe than necessaRy

in the dark of the cemetery behind Grover Cleveland High
she sits on tombstones with friends

smoking Marlboro Reds, harmonizing
Beach Boys

serenading the dead. And like the walking dead
who still yearn for the power of speech,

the school dropout dragging dust
from the old world—finds the L train

to 14th St., and Manhattan's Bleecker St.,
in stained dress, bare feet, peace

and flower painted on her cheek—O Man!
The times they are a-changin', but nothin'

nothin's cool. Who's Rosa Parks? Dr. King?
'NAM?   Who?   Who teaches her

how to tongue kiss at the Village Gate, dance real slow,
who calls her devil with the blue dress on?

Sonnet for a Girl

There's an entrance to a cellar door in Kabul
There are in-laws gripping hand tools with pivoted jaws
Pulling out fingernails from Sahar Gul,
Gangly bride, 13, moaning on piles of hay

There are shocks and aftershocks in the 21st century
That don't come from active volcanoes
Sometimes they come from reading a story
In the week-end *New York Times*

Sahar Gul refused to do laundry today, refused
To cook, refused to lie down with her husband
There's nothing like ear and vagina sizzling
With hot iron to teach this Afghan girl a lesson

Which god officiates these temples of fire?
Same as creates peaceful seas, shelters, clinics?

Pink Moon Child

1.

Prendi, prendi fra le dita quella margherita che ti brucia il cuore
"Take, take between your fingers that daisy that fuels the heart"

The tide rolled me out with music from the radio,
mother singing, pedaling her sewing machine Necchi
churning like a train. We all shared a room. It was the bed where I lay
half awake half walking in fields of tall stemmed daisies. I pulled petals
and longed for my mother: *she loves me, loves me not.*

Daisies, little foot, Necchi's needle stopped. Mamma?
What is that pink zigzag on your lap? My new embroidered pillow?
Tea napkin moon drops? Why does the machine sew
pink sparks?
　　　　Pink is for my pink moon child. Stop asking questions.
Get your head out of the clouds.

I don't like pink pillows, pink dresses or drinking from her glass.
Mezzogiorno—around the table eating and I'm the only one without a glass.
Why does Aldo have hair under his arms and not me? Mamma
who do you love best? Looks stop my swallowing. I shrink.
Her heavy sigh, another sigh, hard blows of breath. I know the moon
burns white, but that music overflows with questions.

2.

Before my first menses
I stopped asking questions.
Love had ceased being greed for that dramatic child.
Father lay dead in pink powder; Mother sat broken in black
inside a Queens funeral parlor
my legs tired of genuflecting near a figure of wax.
The funeral man in broken Italian
said return at 7 for evening prayers to our heavenly father.
Outside the cold and the dark screamed
don't count on any more fathers.

We rolled and painted our pain on walls,
you sighed, sank deeper—*what's the use; we're just*
two helpless … do we leave? Sicily is no place for women.

Necchi still wrapped in heavy blankets from across
the ocean followed us—
hell and back—there's more
than one way
more than one
time we die.
Hawks circled the sky in Central, on Grove, Bleecker,
Long Island, Metropolitan, back to Brooklyn, Queens—
looking out across dirty streets dirty skies
I tried to find a clearing—towards
what? I sighed and sighed.

3.

No bowel movement in ten days. I know accumulated shit
hurts you more than dying. Here I am Mamma,
a tapeworm wanting your petrifying feces. How
can I relieve you?

Where is love today when there is nowhere in this world
I can take you. No unemployment office, hospital, no
Orchard Street for fabrics to embroider, no visits
to the cemetery with your wet washcloth and little shovel
asking Salvatore, *Turiddu, Who?* *Will tend our tombstone?*

We're on the nineteenth mile—Go. Go on.
I once swam helpless in your moist cave,
you breathed   opened   pushed hard so I could see the light,
now we're synchronized in a tempest and I swear God's

been sleeping for a long time. Our chests fly and fall
violently as all our mothers' uterine contractions.

I was once held, now I'm the holder of your hand. See
the clearing? No more fear of loneliness or pain, poverty.
You're weightless, suspended—your hair wavy black

cascades down your back—shiny as caper leaves on walls
of golden tufa. There's the straw hut— *E Maccuni,* the one
Turiddu made—your favorite spot near azure waters,

medlar trees and grape vines. I've taken off your socks;
your feet were always cold on earth. I've painted

your toes red. Go barefoot now and sing of daisies,
colored moons, all the love songs you ever knew. Today
you're the loveliest of women. I'll mourn and mourn tomorrow.

That Jasmine Twig

We snuck it through Customs one year—
that jasmine twig in and out every spring and frost

grew into a lovely shrub, climbed
the lattice we'd made. Flowered even in December.

That jasmine saw the firstborn off to college. For months
I served a pound of pasta that used to feed four.

You and I have dug, watered and tended our transplants
like that jasmine in the pot, now almost a tree outgrown.

The mind drifts and swerves; heart,
accustomed to devotion, wants to jump out of its bowl.

I Wanted to Show You

Toward the end we moved awkwardly to Vivaldi's *Spring*. I caressed you through taut skin to Chopin's *Nocturne Opus Nine*. Only time I'd have you to myself. Dr. Antenucci said late babies love the sound of their mother's heart so much they hold on as long as they can. Labor began on a June morning; I insisted: no drugs. Nurses changed shifts. *You need help,* someone said *forceps.* I whispered *please, a little more time.* You must have sensed the threat—within minutes you turned from sunny-side-up and rushed out, right ear resembling an *orecchietta*—you know, the semolina pasta I make with sausage and broccoli rabe. I thought *Oh God, I can fix that ear*—more Oh Gods as you grew though I claimed not to be religious, but would have made deals: Oh God spare her her father's depression, let her not have sex until she's mature enough to handle it—if that son-of-a-bitch breaks her heart, I'll buy a bat and break his legs. I had been in love before, but not like this—your lips, eyelashes, smell of your skin. Today we sat by Copley Pond like we used to—watched the ducks Ozzie and Harriet glide, heard the sound of water over rocks. You said *Mother, you don't know me.* I wanted to show you, show you my left breast that hangs so much lower than my right. You would only eat from the left—the one nearer the sound of a heart.

Cafeteria Carpet

In this winter half-light the carpet seems a brown field
with scattered fruit droppings.
I sit by the window and enter stains.
That loathing first year in America—
Now here father's blood caked on the bathroom floor
followed us no matter where, no matter
how many times we moved. There
Mother always made sure we had a good working stove.
And I follow our steps where we painted walls,
set stick-on titles on kitchen floors
hoping roaches wouldn't like
the smell of clean.

New World Names & Notions

The Willoughby—Junior High School 162—was no farm by the willow. Not one blade of Brooklyn grass or grammar lesson in that zoo of black and white animals. Guinea and Nigger were the first slurs I learned—convinced they were nicknames like traditions the Southern Italians brought. They called each other Vinny sangu ri porcu (blood of pig), Franky cazzu rossu (swollen dick), Pete piru vugghiutu (boiled pear). All the blacks were Muligna` (eggplant). I think it was Swollen Dick gave me my nickname, Mattisa (I get it up). *Quannu ti viru, Mattisa, Mattisa*—When I see you, I get it up, get it up. How I cried, my name is Marisa, but Mattisa spread like measles, even he who was lean and tall, darker than Japanese eggplant—pitch black lingering night—called me I get it up, and had no clue. His eyes sparkled like moons down the hall, in the classroom, on my way home he leaned close so no one could hear: *Mattisa, Mattisa,* and held up his hand in a funny salute while I ran sulking in my red Mary Janes. But he kept at it in my daydreams and once I drew M&M in a heart pierced by spears. One after-school in the schoolyard as the whites challenged the blacks in handball, I saw the brave man. Blood of pig, sore loser, tried to provoke a fight, called him Fuckface, and towering Eggplant said *Vinny, I wouldn't mess with me brother—high five.* Blood of pig squirmed away. Next day before morning bell the ultimate Serenata Notturna waited for me to find a seat; I slapped him a hard high five—said in my best English my name is Ma-ree-sah, what's yours? *Willie.* Wee-lee, I had a great grandfather my town called Achille cantaru (piss pot). Willie cracked up. It was the first time I smiled at The Willoughby, grin to grin, first look at a man's crotch—quick quick.

Photo of Hunchback Woman on the Battlefield

Crossing Piazza Kalsa where Cala Bay once formed Palermo's port,
the hunchback woman with cane hears the old joke: *First thing
when you get home from work in the evening, give your wife a good
beating, you may not know why you're hitting her, but she certainly does!*
Before her eyes date trees vanish, ground opens ruins, Carthaginians,
Greeks, Normans, Moors, every tribe on the globe praying to gods
of war in every port of the island: *We want this golden bowl of tangerines,
we need receptacles for our seed, feces, a prison for exiles.* Gods oblige, Sapph
exiled, forests erased, rivers dried, chicory thorns thrive on every
blood-crack. The woman with downcast eyes hurries her limping—pass
Magna Graecia's bloodied boots, malnourished dogs and stone monume
sprayed red with *Merda*. The fallen soldiers laugh a good hardy laugh.

III

Transforming the I

Then came the time all "Made in Italy" raged
in Manhattan. Fine restaurants on 57th changed
French to Italian. Barney's on 17th displayed
Giorgio Armani with haloed head. New Yorkers sat outside
Café San Benedetto sipping espresso, pinkies up,
talking the latest Fellini. I bought cigarette jeans
in boutique *La Madonna* when sacraments
went retail. *Jesus Jeans* cost my week's pay
which meant I wouldn't help mother with the rent.
How could I not buy them? A rear pocket declared:
Chi mi Ama mi Segua (All who Love me shall Follow).
Guinea shame had passed. I was chic; I thickened
my accent, got drunk on men who followed my ass.
What did Jesus, to whom I'd prayed so hard
for deliverance, think of the Italian American sheep
stretched belly up in Central Park's dazzling grass?
Maple leaves danced hip-hop in the breeze,
birds spread their wings and interrogated
the rose colored sky. I didn't understand
what they were asking. But for a little while
their songs allowed heart to lift and empty its laments
before retracing my steps to a crumbling Brooklyn tenement
lowering my head, hand over my mouth I entered
the old dark and narrow hallway of the immigrant.

Santuzza, bitter bride, encounters Ms. Alien researching Sicily's 20th century marriage customs

You're wondering why I'm wearing long Saudi Sicilia in my nuptial portrait. The Saracens brought us olive trees, and we extract delicious oil; they brought us veils, and we imprison our souls. I won't speak of other colonizers, how they diminished human freedom for two thousand years and what the indigenous Sicels gained and lost. One story at a time. Ms. Alien, my betrothed's sisters (I'll call them malafruscoli dressed in virtuous veneer in this tale—mutt tyrannicals with horns and pitchforks) suggested I wear green to be their brother's breeder. You're wondering why my beloved never asked for my hand. I had no father, the malafruscoli called my mother fat ass, and he assumed an automatic yes. Why did they scheme and hide a platinum ring inside my birthday cake? To make the bondage appear benevolent and modern, invited me to eat the cake's vanilla sponge and lick the cream until my deadened faculties found the prize. Was I poor beggar receiving the Emir? Ms. Alien, some Sicilian women become afflicted with the sickness—Sicilian Sickness is a form of aphasia that kills every single celebration. Maybe it comes from being in our hot sun too long picking olives when there's little else to eat. I swallowed the bait but was never blind. I knew the dirty little truth about malafruscolo spirit, it resembled mine—I could scarcely keep from unifying. Our culture wages an imbecile's war on women—makes us prick worshippers and the sickness wants to spread.

Sometimes a girl's first love comes on like a disease and symptoms are hives of bad decisions. Amo quia absurdum (I love because it is absurd). Like a maniac I should have kicked my groom in the groin, poured hot pepper seeds down his throat, struggled to get away from his embraces. Now, I want to know myself, so I closely examine my complaints. I'd ask him to make compassion easier. Speak up. Kneel in front of my mother's grave all night and beg permission to cherish her daughter, and persist if she refuses, and quit telling me to relax.

I wanted to drown the flowers, light matches on my skin. Ms. Alien, are you suggesting I eat something sweet to balance my bitterness? I'm surfing waves of emotions. He turned out a noble husband in a thousand ways, you should know—we've made great love together. He stood isolated before my senses, and I saw his intentions. I was all stupid nods and smiles who had empathy for him and his little pig-snouted sisters twitching and snorting at my food. I made the sisters jasmine sachets, tweezed their whiskered chins, massaged their tortured heads, removed thorns from their paws, offered myself as family, but still they didn't sit on my toilet bowl—squatted six metres away, and I've cleaned urine-stained-floors with bleach like serf Pisciarella, and I've sprinkled salt on the corners of the bathroom to sanctify my home.

When I sat to read a book about a woman who does not accept the conditions of her life and sells her soul, the malafruscoli brought minestrone. You would think this a display of camaraderie and affection, but they said here, our brother must be starving. Slowly

I became dismayed, developed an allergy to sweets since the day of cake and cream and soup tasting like the bitterest wormwood herb.

Bitter releases bile, Bitter activates the liver to detoxify, Bitter repairs the stomach's lining and reverses ulcers. Bitter helps heal me from a time I struggled with myself and my malafruscolo culture, kicked the abyss, howled at the moon, and pulled my hair in fistfuls for the right to keep some sense of self alive. In the twenty-first century some Sicilian women refuse marriage, and if lovers and relatives put up a fight, they take the next flight north with a Toc Ferro (piece of iron) in miniskirt pockets for good luck. But you say you want another example of the old disease, let me put it this way:

More Sicilian Sickness

When one sister-in-law said: I'm warning you
comb that wild natty hair or my brother
will leave you—I became gorgon Medusa
whose head of snakes aimed to turn the grand-bitch
to stone. She became an elder holding
my legs open for clitoral mutilation, tossing
holy hood and labia to Dog God
in neighboring Africa—who's eaten 120 million
veri clitoridi. You may guess the other elder
said: we'll take our brother home. She blessed
the excision—knife, scissor, razor.

Ferragosto

How tender I feel, how delicate is life hanging in balance
when noon comes with its smell of tomato sauce rising
like church bells announcing Mass. August 15th,
Ferragosto, when even farmers leave the oven of hills
burnt brown after picking the last green almond.
Everyone hits the beach on the day named for Augustus,
then the Assumption. She'll go out tonight
on a wooden boat trimmed with every heady flower grown
on the island, bless the boats — they'll return to harbor
with plenty of fish. Lady in blue plaster cloak with crown
of metallic stars sways in water well past dark. A million
lit candles float. Sea sky and sky sea — all the stars
in the universe gather in Scoglitti.

I used to talk with magic —
night sea, blue boats, candles replied: Time for Music.
The band plays *Vitti Na Crozza Supra Nu Cannuni*
(I Saw a Skull on Top of a Cannon).
Young and old islanders sing to a skull that cries to be buried —
the loudest voices from women my grandmother calls
black suitcases under bright umbrellas.
I gaze across the ocean — I say hello, farewell, dear lined faces.

Amore Muto

Fall, fall with me
               to the calm ocean floor.
Who needs sea releasing sea scum between toes—
spring blows grit into crevices of your teeth,
noise pollutes jays and robins, garish azaleas
and irises come screaming mating seasons—

Heat will go down, daylight slowly fade;
find what can't be found where I'm flashy loud
and walk on singing foot.
I'm Etna, pizza, mozzarella, mother's heart.

Suck in pain like your mother sucked marrow
from osso buco—thinking it cured her cancer. Stop
resisting the spent flame—tarantella,
mandolins, the *pu ti pu*
and *Cavalleria Rusticana's* blood-feud.

      I'm a little tired of contralti and rioting
      worlds. I want a beginning with no purpose.
      Strip me to the gesture of woman pinching an earring,
      head titled, hands coming together to enter a silent space,
      man behind mirror filling his eyes with her form.
      Fall, fall with me
             to the ocean floor
                  for beauty's sake.

Folle, Furtive Little Night Dream

Hands, my hands kneading biscuit flour,
locks of hair near my eyes you tuck behind one ear.

Moonlight floods your eyes in blue, in blue and snowy
places a doorway opens Paris, *La Boheme*

Ma per fortuna e` una notte di luna, e qui` la luna l'abbiamo vicina
in unbroken sequence the crossing/uncrossing of your knees,

a glance, a look away, a penetrating stare—to Maine's
autumn fields of bittersweet, milkweed, an old tree.

Shift, bend, loop around me—we're pinned to oak
as Augustine is pinned to God. As if shushing a child

your forefinger taps my lips: *Does the fox care about courage,*
cowardice, failure? Nothing comes from dreaming. What of living joy you say

What will I do in summer I ask. Can nothing come from keeping
a piece of sea glass in my mouth as if it were your tongue?

I wake tired of entanglements, tired beyond trembling, still spiraling
in my bed, though you've never held my hand.

The College Boyfriend

No hellos or goodbyes when he came in or left the house;
he read at the kitchen table, curled on my couch to write
before clearing his plate. Well, this must be
the college boyfriend phase; long term she'll choose a man
with social grace, he'll speak Italian, help me take
the garbage out. Dave Koch was mum even when my Mother
died. He looked deep into my eyes, gave me a pocket copy
of *Kaddish*. Next night discs, more Ginsberg, Rukeyser.
I learned more from Dave's eyes—they loved the stars,
my farmer daughter, my sauce marinara. Before he left
for grad school he and my farmer broke house rules, slept
in the same bed. Morning came; I faked again—didn't see
him cry and peel out of the driveway. I never
said goodbye. Funny things college boyfriends—one day here,
five years later sudden death. Your daughter needs
one who speaks. But that boy drove off with pieces
of your heart, left his talking blue eyes by your stove. Upstairs
a white shirt, sweat socks, a black *Moleskine* rubber-banded.

Comma in the Sky

Here I build a bonfire under a comma in the sky, and I will burn
cloth with tightly finished seams keeping us stiff and upright,
shoulder pads that lift us higher than the next guy—
the shimmering buttons, $10 hook and eye shutting
and sealing hearts, the rick-rack serpentine and fringes
suffocating vocal chords. My hands stroking this 7-ply
cashmere really want to hug the goats—want to retract
my hand rolled in fabric bolt, order the grading chalk
to write what the world has lost. Which christening gown
gives our kids the best blessing—which blanket seals bloody
covenants with a tyrant. Which fabric
dipped in poisonberry appeases anger and disdain.
Which timeless classic reinvents boredom with twisted
ribbon, herringbone and pique` soaked in titanium.

Meeting at MoMA

You say I'm among Marlene Dumas's
portraits of measured graves.
Am I the ashen woman with strong thighs
out of eggs and out of business
facing a youthful you with blue erection?
Or Miss Pompadour in black leather boots
waiting to be entered from the back?

Consider

I'm birthing in pain, or rather pain is birthing me
in mucus, blood and symbiosis—
frontal cortex still in bloom sends mixed
signals to that mass of contradiction, heart
sometimes wayward, sometimes rooted,
mostly hidden behind verticals with Madame
Kupka on the fourth floor.

Disposable Goods

Girls are taught to lick
their lips—hold up three
little fingers— say *Yum Yum
Boom Boom—$50 for three*

Business is booming
in this part of Cambodia
rich in commodities
prized   virginal

delicate treats
some so small
they barely reach
their customers' belts

Bloody vaginas stitched
over and over and over
*Yum Yum Boom Boom
$50 for three*

Raffaela at Eighteen

Raffaela hid under the olivewood
        Farmtable made by ancestor sweat—

Squeezed hard her ears and legs
        But the bombs, the dread, the labor pain
Could not hold her firstborn in

He flew out from under the table's woodgrain
        Weighed less than a head of cabbage

Raffaela later said her boy resembled a ferret—
        Hair covered all except palms and soles

Her husband kept the runt swaddled in gauze and total darkness
        Inside a cotton-covered dresser drawer

When his eyes rested—a moment of freeze—he asked his wife
        What is this thing?

More bombs fell on Vittoria's rooftops—
        Stampedes and shrills stormed dust-clouded streets

Mediterranean sea lanes opened for an Allied Armada of 2,590
And The US Liberty hit by enemy bombers exploded off Gela in 1943

Raffaela's back let down, but her silk-soft nipples could not
                    Coax the limp mouth to eat

Some neighbors abandoned their homes, others sought shelter
                    Through half swung doors

Raffaela sat silent and cross-legged, keeping vigil by the drawer

Eventually she rose
                    There was sunlight in the courtyard

And a German rifle tracking movement from a tree

                    All Raffaela could do is urge and urge
The bitch with litter—
                    Could she borrow one hungry pup?

Could it suck and suck until blood oozed

Until its teeth erected her human nipples like cathedrals?

All she knew is somewhere a world away was no mania to destroy
But to feed—none whimpered and whined from hunger

Women drew water from wells to quench a stranger's thirst —
Garlic, onion, drying figs hung on kitchen walls

Somewhere frugal hands mended socks and celebrated love —
Infants nursed and slept in cradles

Wind carried sounds from nearby villages
Of men and women churning wheat

And delicate saffron crocus poked through black lava,
Orange calendula grew in open fields

Where cows with thick hides and swollen udders
Shook away bullet-ridden parachutes

And falling bombs
Like flies

Quannu Chiuveva Petali Russi e Aranciuni

Chista e' l'ultima fotografia nta' lu studio di me patri:
Matri, Patri, Aldo, iu cu magghia d'angora a filu doratu.

Prima ca l'obbiettivu scattau, affiraiu li so manu,

chidda di idda vicinu lu me pettu, chidda di iddu chiu' vicunu la me facc
Sapennu ca m'avissi bisugnatu ssu mumentu prima di New York,
quannu avevu vogghia d'acchianari grattacieli.

Parti di me stissa arristau 'nta l'isola di alivi e pruna, currennu
cu iddu tra collini Ragusani quannu chiuveva petali russi e aranciuni—
acchiappavu

petali di papaviri cu li manu e la lingua—arristaiu assittata nta' la
Vespa virdi puma

menzu li so rinocchia, me Matri d'arreri cu lu prendisoli sciuratu
e fazzulettu azzurru n' testa sbatteva cu lu ventu, e Aldo appinnuluni

cu lu fanalinu di cura—diritti versu lu mari Scugghitti.
Schugghitti, unni la famigghia era ancora una e iu appartinevu,

sana, riconuscibbili come lu nostru pizzuddu di Mediterraniu.

When it Rained Red and Orange Petals

This is the last photograph of us in father's studio:
Mother, Father, Aldo, me in angora sweater with Lurex thread.

Before the camera flashed I grabbed their hands,

hers close to my chest, his nearer my face. I would need that moment
before New York City, when I longed to climb skyscrapers.

Part of me remained behind on that island of olives and plums running
with him in *Ragusani* hills—when it rained red and orange poppy petals—

I caught them with my hands and my tongue—forever sit

on his apple green Vespa, hunched low below his knees, Mother behind him
in a flowered dress, blue head scarf beating in the wind, and Aldo

hanging with the tail light headed for the beach *Scoglitti.*
Scoglitti, where we were still one, and I belonged somewhere,

whole, familiar as our piece of Mediterranean.

New Wine in November

Summer fields burnt brown from too many scalding
        suns, too little rain, turn green in November
as fiddleheads I forage in spring on the North Fork.
        My body here, mind like tightly wrapped fern
on volcanic earth when fieldwork was done and vines
        shed leaves for winter sleep.
Grapes in vats convert into nectar for gods every November
        for the feast of San Martino.
Mother makes biscotti hard as week-old bread with hints
        of anise seeds—a poor man's sweet for a poor man's
saint—*poor things define a civilization* she'd say.
        Her hand on the handle of a perforated
metal pan shakes foraged chestnuts roasting
        on the stove, and Father opens a bottle of Novello,
drink it tonight or it will go bad.
        I remain a moment longer for the bread and wine.
Around a farmtable four glasses lift: "Viva! Pane, Vino e San Martino"
        so fruity, slightly fizzy, biscotti hard
and we dip them in new wine. The gods won't be the only ones
        full as the moon, and drunk tonight.

E Lucevan Le Stelle

Stars among verses
Usher him in
Taciturn
Somber
Searching for a spot
To take me
Gently
There—
Closer to shore
Where salty air
And moonlight
Lure me
Out of character
As I do this
And that
To him
Who is little more
Than half my age
And doesn't know
Opera
At all

Filament Yarns

Were probably first made in a cave
Someone holding a handful of fur
From a dead animal

Interlaced   interlooped
Twisted hair fiber between her fingers
To form a continuous strand

Some yarns are thin as human hair
Supple as my slip
Some are stiff and coarse

Our emotional differences
Two sets of yarns—woven—and sometimes
Every filament in the yarn breaks

Ars Poetica

& Now I live here:
I like vodka straight
My cigarette strong
Expanding my lungs
No wearing Armani
I'm no longer a type
No eating with fork
& knife—My family
Dear friends—I've
Dribbled away—Oh
Lord—living unclean
Like a hen's feather
In a chicken's coop
I slip slither & slide
Like molten lava
In a dirty pajama—
Pulse in moonmist
Behind the blue blade
Hide in Dante's
Dense & deep forest
Should anyone call
!Say—gone fishing
In oceans of mystery
!Say there's no-way
In this ruling world
Of reviving the fool
Only the living are
Still possessed with
What the living do

IV

Via Incanto

There's a path in the woods
Whose voice I know
It's always been there
The song with long arms

Stritti Stritti Comu Sempri

Cert'uni nasciuti cca cammisa,
Cert'uni cca suttana   cert'uni nuri e cruri
Pirmittitimi amici mei

Mettu in carta oggi
Lu duviri ca v'aspetta:

Sunatimi A Traviata
Chiu` forti ca putiti,
Nuddu comu vui lu po` capiri
Comu mi   facia trimari

Celebbrati cu buttigghia di Prosecco
E jazz a la Siciliana ca rumpi gammmi alli seggi

E l'ura scappata
Ripurtira` piaciri
Di tutti li nostri virgili di C'apu D'anno

Quannu veni l'ura di chiuriri lu tabbutu e vurricarmi
Vurricati puru li me sicaretti e li cirini

Termus cu cafe` ristrittu   non troppu azzuccaratu

Sciascia e Pirandellu

Tight Tight Like Always

Some born with a shirt on
Some with a slip   some naked and raw
Permit me my friends

I put the duty that awaits you
Down on paper:

Play *La Traviata*
Loud as you can
No one but you can understand
How it   made me tremble

Celebrate with a good Prosecco
& Sicilian jazz breaking chair legs

The fleeting hour
Will recall pleasures
Of our spent midnights

When it's time to close the box
Bury my cigarettes and matches with me

Thermos with espresso made short   not too sweet

Sciascia and Pirandello

Un fallu   ubbidienti e forti   ppi passarimi n'anticchia e tempu
Dui coccia 'i pumaroru ppi la sarsa   chiddi abbummuliddu e profumati
Pampini di basilico` se li truvati

Nun vi scurdati lu vostru affettu
L'aneddu di lu me sposo ca m'ha saputo amari
Lu sciavuru de me figghi
Quann' eranu picciriddi

*

Quannu veni lu vostru turnu —
Vucchi arrappati e codda assitati
Nun sacciu ancora 'nta quali stidda o diminsioni mi truvati
Ma sapiti ca v'aspettu cu vrazza aperti
Musica abbunnanti   la tavula cunsata

A phallus   obedient and strong   for me to pass a little time
A few tomatoes to make sauce   the plum sweet smelling kind
Basil leaves   if you find them that time of year

Don't forget your affection
My beloved's ring
My children's smell when they were just
Little things

                    *

When your turn comes—
Mouths shriveled and throats parched
I don't yet know star or dimension
But know I'll be waiting
With open arms   table set   music blasting

Braided Tree

for my daughters

First stars already shining
above Iblean hills,

through the white hawthorn
our ancestors called butcher's broom

the wind murmurs and goes
as I read tales from the Brothers Grimm.

There, under the tree braided
with branches in bloom

is the nest of young dreams.
Even then I could see myself

on a journey of search,
of what would be you.

Catena in Black Shawl

Listen carefully my daughters:
this is a photograph of my great-grandmother Catena. Her name
means Chain. She sits on caned chair in front of our door on Via Bixio.
She sits like the palest wash of stone shrouded in black,
cleaning sardines. How does she emit so much light?
We must all know ourselves through our known
and unknown mothers strapped to our chests.
In the 21st century we look men in the eye—we work
for pay and buy and fry sardines
from Portugal, sit round a table and nod
to each other. We work and buy and tend
house with its flower garden, and the fig tree survives.
We pass our clipped wings to you—

Listen carefully American daughters, stay
in school, and join us when these old
tambourines coax our fingers to play—

Black Madonna of Tindari drawn on the drum,
release Raffaela, Giovanna,
Maria, Delizia, Catena out of Siculo Inferno—

Drum, beat, drum the *pizzicata*,
sting *tarantula tarantata tarantella* tracking our cries,
shaking our voices—dissolve, devour evil spirits.

Our stolen spirits, white skirts, red sashes with eyes ears mouth
feet and hands do a little fancy dancing. In whirlwind
fury and sound, in conversation with death
enters the force—the dance—dance to tarantula poison—
poison Get *out* of our blood, enemy and accomplice.

We work and buy and stuff whole sardines
Sicilian style—*beccafico*—breadcrumbs, raisins,
lemon rind, pinch of sugar, spoonful of vinegar,
bay leaf between each one—round our table
we nod to each other—and we laugh
when Catena says maybe those men
needed to eat more sardines—

Canto for a Quilter

earliest surviving quilted coverlet

I want to name you Cantacutra, say your offering is not lost.
Your Tristan quilt hangs on a museum wall. We marvel
at the faces, the cotton corded knights in battle, how tight
the *trapuntato* stitch, eight to ten per inch.

How abandoned your lovers in relief medallion of rolling hills
& fields of fleur des lis. Who kissed you, Cantacutra?
Did the brave knight lift your heart as you knotted, twisted
threads into Sicilian verse? *Tristaiunu dai lu guantu*

Tristaiunu a tradimantu sings your needle upward,
downward, as Iacopo da Lentini sang with ink and feather.
I seem to be forever watching you pour life
into a coat of arms, eyes transfixed on Tristan folded on your lap

as you stitch and backstitch into the passing centuries—linen
threads of cream & white—for someone else's wedding night.

Petra Panayotis

Your speech is blurred; right eye drooped and bruised
makes those long lashes look purple, straighter.

I was once an eagle now I'm a chicken you laugh, joke
about a fly that acquired an ass and shit on the entire world.

I wonder what your face will look like next month,
how your body will shrink and no longer guide me

to swim in Elafonisos, reach the white church, pick white lilies
off the sand. How long before you can't hold a book,

can't swallow? Maybe I can read to you every day for an hour,
The Illiad—and take you to Sicily's Aeolian Islands named for

the god of winds. Will you hold the scent of earth
after rain when you're laid up in the downstairs guestroom.

When sight is last to go, can I scribble in your eyes.
Thank you for calling me *sister, una faccia una razza,*

never phoning, just showing up with wine, grilled pita
and mullets. I'll read to you every day for an hour, find a way

back to you Panayotis, holy bread, most beautiful rock I know.

The Water Episode

Pellegrino bottle sweating soft between my thighs—

May I have a drink of water?

My sunglasses lowered—I look up—

All that thirst where his eyes fixed
All that color beginning at once at the base of his neck

I want to say
Spend the rest of your life with me as you are
Blushing like the sunset on my thighs—

May I have a drink of water?

Force that lights our free play
In the violet hour
Framed in floating shapes, smooth

Hand cupping breast, foot arched—
Arms lifted toward paradise—
A few centimeters yet

Divide our mouths
In a beautifully molded shadow wearing quicksilver
Leaving his sunfish and falling over my beach chair

Did I live or die that summer moment?

(And the forbidden man
Did break and burn under his hat)

Was I garland-crowned nymph
Changed to flowing spring in his escape?

Were we on a North Fork dune
Or palm-fringed Siracusa
As Fonte Cyane running into River Anapus?

May I have a drink of water?

I quickly focused on a gull feather   little sticks   little rocks
Shoulders stooped   head bent   hands hung limp
Bottle rolled on stilted sand
Chair turned to stone to calm my frightened soul

Athena to a Dreamer

Deep in a teak Adirondack chair,
Day after day transfixed
On the white sail, the last dark wave —

How can the mariner return,
Make his way home to you
Penelope, climbing the sky of stars,
To a landbreeze he's never known?

Get a move on, old girl,
Your husband of all seasons
Waits day after day
With warm steel-cut oats
Currants   Quinoa   Amaranth
Real maple syrup from Vermont.

Aurora

The sun comes up molten gold
Over Peconic Bay—
Over this glass house of dawns—

Another cunning dawn
Takes revenge
And I look down at my hands

Soon too frail to write poems
Catch the rain, hair
Too thin to splay on a lover's pillow

And otherness comes down hard:
Where have you been hiding
Dark feminine of the moon?

Who is this I? Who is this you?

The Emerald Dress

Emerald as Puget Sound was Celestina's dress
for the black tie affair on the sprawling lawn—
raw silk shantung, shoulder blades exposed,
not yet old, V slimming waist,
chestnut hair fixed high, but soft and loose—
a few curls escaped to the neck like whispers
he'd follow, would not resist kissing. The pockets
gaped in slight poof—concealing hands that had wrung
out the veins since his long absence. Face him!
Underwire: support the body to stand, breasts:
act as doves, suggest peace—breathe
soothingly, deeply, and wait for a triumphant beginning.
How would he see her when the sun set,
would it prove too late? Bare arms glowed amber—
an enchantress Undine rising out of the sea
in a luminous Botticelli? He once called her Sea Legs.
But no—all mermaids did was circle and wait
to kill sailors—not the best job. Long ago
rummaging through a yard sale on some country lane,
they bought two tablecloths for a song, original wrap,
one red/white check, one blue/white—one man's refuse
is another man's treasure he said, and out of nowhere,
she personified grace itself. The most sublime song
could do her no justice—how could her heart
keep up with all he'd said about her in his songs.

She was ready to dance to a full Tchakovsky orchestra
as Odotte anticipating Prince Siegfried when she turned
to face *gray hair at temples, shoulders a little more stooped; he could use*
a good tailor, and he's taller than I remember — *Oh God*
introductions — *his new flame.* How lucky
for sunglasses hiding the whites of eyes turning
crimson, and the dress and wine etherizing while
a greenish worm slobbers inside, slobbers unloved,
and waiters drop trays, bottles, glasses on the open bar
shatter. The poised silhouette in emerald dress
says *Pleasure* — Undine, Odette, even the doves, say good
Celestina you skipped the jewelry. Nothing takes away
from you in that dress. Nothing can disguise you
from yourself. Now walk and sit indifferent.

When All Grew Silent

Black gold my father calls coffee he downs
like a whiskey shot, says best things in life
are bitter at the top, and croons the old song
I'll turn and twist you little cup, till sugar
sweetens my mouth. He winks at my mother.

After lunch & coffee everything pauses.
Lazy like immobile birds
with slit eyes on the fig tree — we file inside
for naps. Too hot, no breeze on the patio,
scalded asphalt burns holes in your shoes.

When night flowers open purple trumpets
we wake, when bougainvillea blazes blue-red
on the roof like a comforting blanket, when night
softens sky of those summer days,
father puts on a clean shirt, mother a sundress.

Her most beautiful is black like her hair —
poppies not wilted swath me in excess
sensation. It was a time of no scarcity, except
running water. But the bathtub was full &
the *Moka* pot dipped *always* before washing

your face. And oh god it's wonderful
to get out of bed, wash your face in the morning

with running water.

                    But standing here
in suburbia, looking at grey slants of snowy light

I'm on my third cup— turn, twist & taste
tormenting cold & wait for evening, for morning,
nothing more bitter than waiting for phone to ring,
email to ping— nothing of a time when nothing
meant life & color of sky & a walk in the piazza.

In this rustling hum of Northern Blvd.,
hand reaches for those motherly eyes, fatherly arms
no lover can match. And heart beats stronger as I graze
bottom of my cup
                    fractal pattern of dried out river.

Don Paolo's Myth

The widow scryer shunned by the town
came to our studio with single photo in hand,
gazed into it as if it were a crystal ball — *Spiritus
Mundi*, she said, and crossed herself. Don Paolo
had died without toll of a bell, snapped
his self portrait, she couldn't fathom how —
paralyzed so many years. He'd run a small
brothel back of his barbershop when houses
were set on fire — allowed by laws of the 2nd war.
He'd fed Ninuzza, who slept off afternoons
on a piss soaked mattress, with canned beef
stolen from the Allies and the Germans busy
getting blowjobs for two lira. The widow
had faith Signor Frasca could erase signs
of syphilis, peel back the miles of life's layers,
stick Paolo's tongue hanging right side
of his mouth back in. Make his smile, restore
no-sin soft to his eyes as when in youth
we're less practiced at self presentation. Fresh
cut flowers would frame Paolo in medallion
mounted on marble headstone — she'd lock
eyes with a gentleman — dance her heart out
under a shady cypress though her hair had
thinned and body hardened and filled out. Year
after year she had cut and rolled her hair into balls

like yarn, sold her best feature for a Carrara
slab, moscato wine she'd spill onto the earth,
quench Paolo's thirst, if Signor Frasca guaranteed
the polished oval would not fade in any weather,
she had good money to pay for a Second Coming.

September Equinox

You'll come
between sunset and moonrise, when a star orders earth to skip darkness.

I'll arrange blue aster for the table, offer eggplants cut lengthwise,
thick and fried, sprinkle parmigiano, drape the poplars in tulle,

light a thousand quince-scented candles, and the lake, the lake
will glow amber from a harvest moon. Seeing you will be so good,

as will that smelly little crab and sea glass you leave again
in friendship on the bench outside my porch. I will give them back

to the sea—as if they were your ashes—after I see you
one last time.

Ask the Sun for a Face of Petals

Mind in the clouds—head bending
to smell a rose on the verge of summer—
losing all the torments—
how hard I'm wishing 700 million
kilowatts from the sun return me
to a sea rose unconnected to past things

My spiny stems chase away sand crabs—
my wrinkled leaves keep rabbits
from their midnight snacks—
I'm unconcerned with endangered ospreys
Sicily or Quebec—my blooms
will wither with the approaching frost

Only love won't leave me alone—
I still see the black pincushion sea
holding stars—love when youth
when love was moon
when I kicked off my shoes
by the lowlands of a faraway slow river

Marisa Frasca is co-founder of Magia, Inc., an Italian children's clothing firm she ran for twenty-seven years. She is also a poet and translator whose work has appeared in *5 AM, Philadelphia Poets, Adanna Journal, Voices in Italian Americana, Sicilia Parra, Feile-Festa, Sweet Lemons II,* and other literary journals and anthologies. She was named first runner-up for the 2013 National Bordighera Poetry Prize for this book, *Via Incanto,* judged by distinguished poet Lia Purpura.

Frasca was a Riggio fellow and scholar at The New School where she earned a BA in Creative Writing; she also holds an MFA in poetry from Drew University. She serves on the executive board of The Italian American Studies Association, The Italian American Writers Association, and the advisory board of *Arba Sicula*—an organization that preserves and disseminates Sicilian literature and folklore. Born in Vittoria, Italy, Frasca now resides in Manhattan and Long Island's North Fork.

VIA FOLIOS

A refereed book series dedicated to the culture of Italians and Italian Americans.

DOUG GLADSTONE. *Carving a Niche for Himself* Vol 95 History. $12

MARIA TERRONE. *Eye to Eye* Vol 94 Poetry. $15

CONSTANCE SANCETTA. *Here in Cerchio* Vol 93 Local History. $15

MARIA MAZZIOTTI GILLAN. *Ancestors' Song* Vol 92 Poetry. $14

DARRELL FUSARO. *What if Godzilla Just Wanted a Hug?* Vol ? Essays. $TBA

MICHAEL PARENTI. *Waiting for Yesterday: Pages from a Street Kid's Life.* Vol 90 Memoir. $15

ANNIE LANZILOTTO, *Schistsong*, Vol. 89. Poetry, $15

EMANUEL DI PASQUALE, *Love Lines*, Vol. 88. Poetry, $10

CAROSONE & LOGIUDICE. *Our Naked Lives.* Vol 87 Essays. $15

JAMES PERICONI. *Strangers in a Strange Land: A Survey of Italian-Language American Books.* Vol. 86. Book History. $24

DANIELA GIOSEFFI, *Escaping La Vita Della Cucina*, Vol. 85. Essays & Creative Writing. $22

MARIA FAMÀ, *Mystics in the Family*, Vol. 84. Poetry, $10

ROSSANA DEL ZIO, *From Bread and Tomatoes to Zuppa di Pesce "Ciambotto"*, Vol. 83. $15

LORENZO DELBOCA, *Polentoni*, Vol. 82. Italian Studies, $15

SAMUEL GHELLI, *A Reference Grammar*, Vol. 81. Italian Language. $36

ROSS TALARICO, *Sled Run*, Vol. 80. Fiction. $15

FRED MISURELLA, *Only Sons*, Vol. 79. Fiction. $14

FRANK LENTRICCHIA, *The Portable Lentricchia*, Vol. 78. Fiction. $16

RICHARD VETERE, *The Other Colors in a Snow Storm*, Vol. 77. Poetry. $10

GARIBALDI LAPOLLA, *Fire in the Flesh*, Vol. 76 Fiction & Criticism. $25

GEORGE GUIDA, *The Pope Stories*, Vol. 75 Prose. $15

ROBERT VISCUSI, *Ellis Island*, Vol. 74. Poetry. $28

ELENA GIANINI BELOTTI, *The Bitter Taste of Strangers Bread*, Vol. 73, Fiction, $24

PINO APRILE, *Terroni*, Vol. 72, Italian Studies, $20

EMANUEL DI PASQUALE, *Harvest*, Vol. 71, Poetry, $10

ROBERT ZWEIG, *Return to Naples*, Vol. 70, Memoir, $16

AIROS & CAPPELLI, *Guido*, Vol. 69, Italian/American Studies, $12

FRED GARDAPHÉ, *Moustache Pete is Dead! Long Live Moustache Pete!*, Vol. 67, Literature/Oral History, $12

PAOLO RUFFILLI, *Dark Room/Camera oscura*, Vol. 66, Poetry, $11

HELEN BAROLINI, *Crossing the Alps*, Vol. 65, Fiction, $14

COSMO FERRARA, *Profiles of Italian Americans*, Vol. 64, Italian Americana, $16

GIL FAGIANI, *Chianti in Connecticut*, Vol. 63, Poetry, $10

BASSETTI & D'ACQUINO, *Italic Lessons*, Vol. 62, Italian/American Studies, $10

CAVALIERI & PASCARELLI, Eds., *The Poet's Cookbook*, Vol. 61, Poetry/Recipes, $12

EMANUEL DI PASQUALE, *Siciliana*, Vol. 60, Poetry, $8

NATALIA COSTA, Ed., *Bufalini*, Vol. 59, Poetry. $18.

RICHARD VETERE, *Baroque*, Vol. 58, Fiction. $18.

LEWIS TURCO, *La Famiglia/The Family*, Vol. 57, Memoir, $15

NICK JAMES MILETI, *The Unscrupulous*, Vol. 56, Humanities, $20

BASSETTI, ACCOLLA, D'AQUINO, *Italici: An Encounter with Piero Bassetti*, Vol. 55, Italian Studies, $8

GIOSE RIMANELLI, *The Three-legged One*, Vol. 54, Fiction, $15

Bordighera Press is an imprint of Bordighera, Incorporated, an independently owned not-for-profit scholarly organization that has no legal affiliation with the University of Central Florida or with The John D. Calandra Italian American Institute, Queens College/CUNY.

CHARLES KLOPP, *Bele Antiche Stòrie*, Vol. 53, Criticism, $25

JOSEPH RICAPITO, *Second Wave*, Vol. 52, Poetry, $12

GARY MORMINO, *Italians in Florida*, Vol. 51, History, $15

GIANFRANCO ANGELUCCI, *Federico F.*, Vol. 50, Fiction, $15

ANTHONY VALERIO, *The Little Sailor*, Vol. 49, Memoir, $9

ROSS TALARICO, *The Reptilian Interludes*, Vol. 48, Poetry, $15

RACHEL GUIDO DE VRIES, *Teeny Tiny Tino's Fishing Story*, Vol. 47, Children's Literature, $6

EMANUEL DI PASQUALE, *Writing Anew*, Vol. 46, Poetry, $15

MARIA FAMÀ, *Looking For Cover*, Vol. 45, Poetry, $12

ANTHONY VALERIO, *Toni Cade Bambara's One Sicilian Night*, Vol. 44, Poetry, $10

EMANUEL CARNEVALI, Dennis Barone, Ed., *Furnished Rooms*, Vol. 43, Poetry, $14

BRENT ADKINS, et al., Ed., *Shifting Borders, Negotiating Places*, Vol. 42, Proceedings, $18

GEORGE GUIDA, *Low Italian*, Vol. 41, Poetry, $11

GARDAPHÈ, GIORDANO, TAMBURRI, *Introducing Italian Americana*, Vol. 40, Italian/American Studies, $10

DANIELA GIOSEFFI, *Blood Autumn/Autunno di sangue*, Vol. 39, Poetry, $15/$25

FRED MISURELLA, *Lies to Live by*, Vol. 38, Stories, $15

STEVEN BELLUSCIO, *Constructing a Bibliography*, Vol. 37, Italian Americana, $15

ANTHONY JULIAN TAMBURRI, Ed., *Italian Cultural Studies 2002*, Vol. 36, Essays, $18

BEA TUSIANI, *con amore*, Vol. 35, Memoir, $19

FLAVIA BRIZIO-SKOV, Ed., *Reconstructing Societies in the Aftermath of War*, Vol. 34, History, $30

TAMBURRI, et al., Eds., *Italian Cultural Studies 2001*, Vol. 33, Essays, $18

ELIZABETH G. MESSINA, Ed., *In Our Own Voices*, Vol. 32, Italian/American Studies, $25

STANISLAO G. PUGLIESE, *Desperate Inscriptions*, Vol. 31, History, $12

HOSTERT & TAMBURRI, Eds., *Screening Ethnicity*, Vol. 30, Italian/American Culture, $25

G. PARATI & B. LAWTON, Eds., *Italian Cultural Studies*, Vol. 29, Essays, $18

HELEN BAROLINI, *More Italian Hours*, Vol. 28, Fiction, $16

FRANCO NASI, Ed., *Intorno alla Via Emilia*, Vol. 27, Culture, $16

ARTHUR L. CLEMENTS, *The Book of Madness & Love*, Vol. 26, Poetry, $10

JOHN CASEY, et al., *Imagining Humanity*, Vol. 25, Interdisciplinary Studies, $18

ROBERT LIMA, *Sardinia/Sardegna*, Vol. 24, Poetry, $10

DANIELA GIOSEFFI, *Going On*, Vol. 23, Poetry, $10

ROSS TALARICO, *The Journey Home*, Vol. 22, Poetry, $12

EMANUEL DI PASQUALE, *The Silver Lake Love Poems*, Vol. 21, Poetry, $7

JOSEPH TUSIANI, *Ethnicity*, Vol. 20, Poetry, $12

JENNIFER LAGIER, *Second Class Citizen*, Vol. 19, Poetry, $8

FELIX STEFANILE, *The Country of Absence*, Vol. 18, Poetry, $9

PHILIP CANNISTRARO, *Blackshirts*, Vol. 17, History, $12

LUIGI RUSTICHELLI, Ed., *Seminario sul racconto*, Vol. 16, Narrative, $10

LEWIS TURCO, *Shaking the Family Tree*, Vol. 15, Memoirs, $9

LUIGI RUSTICHELLI, Ed., *Seminario sulla drammaturgia*, Vol. 14, Theater/Essays, $10

FRED GARDAPHÈ, *Moustache Pete is Dead! Long Live Moustache Pete!*, Vol. 13, Oral Literature, $10

JONE GAILLARD CORSI, *Il libretto d'autore*, 1860–1930, Vol. 12, Criticism, $17

HELEN BAROLINI, *Chiaroscuro: Essays of Identity*, Vol. 11, Essays, $15

PICARAZZI & FEINSTEIN, Eds., *An African Harlequin in Milan*, Vol. 10, Theater/Essays, $15

JOSEPH RICAPITO, *Florentine Streets & Other Poems*, Vol. 9, Poetry, $9

FRED MISURELLA, *Short Time*, Vol. 8, Novella, $7

NED CONDINI, *Quartettsatz*, Vol. 7, Poetry, $7

ANTHONY JULIAN TAMBURRI, Ed. *Fuori: Essays by Italian/American Lesbians and Gays*, Vol. 6,

Essays, $10

ANTONIO GRAMSCI, P. Verdicchio, Trans. & Intro. , *The Southern Question*, Vol. 5, Social
Criticism, $5

DANIELA GIOSEFFI, *Word Wounds & Water Flowers*, Vol. 4, Poetry, $8

WILEY FEINSTEIN, *Humility's Deceit: Calvino Reading Ariosto Reading Calvino*, Vol. 3,
Criticism, $10

PAOLO A. GIORDANO, Ed., *Joseph Tusiani: Poet, Translator, Humanist*, Vol. 2, Criticism, $25

ROBERT VISCUSI, *Oration Upon the Most Recent Death of Christopher Columbus*, Vol. 1, Poetry,
$3

CPSIA information can be obtained
at www.ICGtesting.com
Printed in the USA
FSOW01n1506150814
3035FS